the wolf & her moon

Louve -ch

in this
with you,
    i share my soul.
for my words
are my magic. -ch

TRIGGER WARNING
&
SELF-CARE REMINDER

in the many pages before you
lay the stories of my life,
my experiences and words
may be triggering.
if you experience feelings arising from past trauma that
do not feel manageable or safe- please stop reading.
if you choose to continue to read,
read with a healthy supportive person nearby
or with a therapist.
the following page also lists self-soothing and grounding
skills to help you with practicing self-care whilst reading.
this book contains topics of:

> mental health, child abuse, sexual assault, suicide, self-harm, bullying, alcoholism, trauma, grief, sex, death, hospitalization, and lgbtq topics.

remember there is no such thing as a trigger-free world, so
please practice self-care before, while, and after reading.

adolescent crisis/suicide intervention

& counseling nineline
1-800-999-9999

LGBTQ national hotline
1-888-843-4564

SELF-SOOTHING & GROUNDING SKILLS

self-soothing skills are used when you feel
emotionally or physically overwhelmed.
try calming aromatherapy, drinking tea, taking a warm
bath or shower, meditating, wrapping yourself in a blanket
or snuggling a friendly animal.

grounding skills are used when you are feeling
triggered, distressed, emotionally overwhelmed, or mentally
removed from the present moment.
to come down from this focus on something that
shocks the senses.
only one sense at a time – try holding a frozen orange,
closing your eyes and focusing on sounds around you,
touching something with a lot of texture or rubbing a gem
stone while focusing on touch, aromatherapy (invigorating
smell), or lighting your favorite candle.

CONTENTS

ACKNOWLEDGMENTS

i want to thank my two dogs who put up with my endless
writing days. my friends and family who inspired me to
get better and to use poetry as my therapy. thank you,
nicole errico, for all the beautiful illustrations and allison
hartje for editing the entire book. i also want to thank
everyone who supported me on this journey; including
my followers on instagram who made me feel my words
found a home in their hearts as well.
thank you.

1 RAISED BY A WOLF

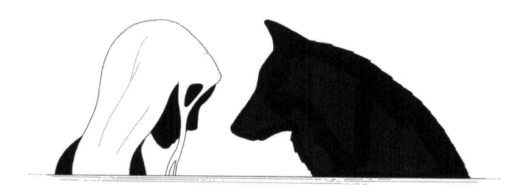

a broken home,
broken bones,
a broken child
who still smiles
because this is all
she's ever known.

arctic wolf.

the day i was born
innocent snow
laced the earth
frosty white.

just like snow,
the innocence
i graced the earth with,
was only fleeting.
a champagne toast
to celebrate my life
how suiting
for it was
my parent's alcoholism
that brought our lives
crumbling down

why can't the snow
stay white?
must all beautiful things
come to dark and violent ends?

i never quite fit in
always different
a wolf hidden
among
a flock of sheep.

all i am
is a frightened little girl
in wolf's clothing.

what it's like for me when you are never there...
i fall asleep on bar floors while you drink
a bed for a child no one bothers to think
my stomach growls in hunger
while you lay in hangovers slumber
i spend my days playing alone
while you pour another shot of patron
i grew up at four years old
because there was no longer an adult hand to hold
it hurts to look back and remember
especially when for you, it's all but a blur
sometimes you'd kiss me goodnight
but i knew the alcohol on your breath means
there will likely be a fight.
one of us ends up black and blue
my mom lies, saying she never knew,
despite me always running to protect her
you may have forgotten, but i remember,
i remember.

wherever you find me,
you will find wolves.

my wolf was always beside me
my copilot through the darkness
he never hurt me like my parents
his chest a pillow as i fell asleep
on cold floors far from home
my guardian angel
i grew up finding
no comfort in human touch
i will always choose my wolf pack
for they are the only ones
who truly know
unconditional love.

mankind's best friend.

he is my lighthouse,
guiding me
through the rocky waters
back to shore.
he is my beacon of hope,
when days are darkest
his love knows no limits.
so i follow his love home
to an endless warm embrace.
unconditional love like no other,
we are linked at the soul.
    - *howling together*

when your parents
can't take care of themselves,
consumed with demons
they never dealt.
how scary it felt
to take the world on as a child,
all the pain you bear seems mild.
you had no other option
but to be strong and take care of them.
learning how to survive again and again,
in the process you never figured out how to live
& somehow, it's yourself you can never forgive.

vices

alcohol wasn't my parents' only vice
drugs stole their souls too
as they used my childhood innocence
as a charade to smuggle drugs across borders.
sometimes i wonder
if i was ever truly their daughter
or was i just a cheap magic trick,
a means to an end.

neglected
how do you learn to love
when your parents' love
resides in the bottom of a barrel
their screams were your lullabies
you search for validation in this world
never finding it the way you want
no one understands you
you're too complicated
you'll never be good enough
doomed to fail from the womb.
i'll tell you this,
life is what you make of it.
release yourself from the shackles
of others' failure and self-hate
because hating yourself
will only keep you trapped
in a cage you can never escape
making your mind into a rabid wolf
oh, how it hurts to be kind to yourself
when all you have ever known is pain
but slowly
you'll etch away the self-loathful scars
that have misshaped your mind
slowly you'll see the beauty in all that you are
in all that you have survived
soon you'll see the love
you have been looking for in others
you can find in yourself
and that love makes life worth living
you have always been
all you have ever needed
believe in yourself
love yourself
fill your world with the love
you know
you deserve
because no one can take that away from you
and no one can ever break you again.

my dad was the first person
to teach me how to break a heart.
now it's my specialty.

~~paging a cardiac surgeon~~

when i look in to my eyes,
i see yours.
when my blood burns,
i feel you running rampant through my veins.
i keep your devilish charm
at arm's length,
protecting others from
pieces of you
that will always be,
in the darkest pieces of me.
every day i fight you,
your wicked ways
will not become mine.
i can't fight DNA.
but i can nurture
my nature,
in ways you never did,
in ways you never would,
Dad.

i watched my world turn to dust,
a family for you just wasn't for us.
despite all your lies and abuse,
i forgive you, let's call it a truce.
you're dead now,
free of your demons despite breaking your vow,
to be a father, to love me, to live forever.
alcohol made you lose your tether
drugs turned you to a monster
but all i ever wanted from you
was to love me as your daughter.

they keep telling me to "feel my emotions"
there is a great sadness in the fact
that the life i have lived
makes it so simple to turn off my emotions
yet so impossibly hard to feel them at all.
my safe space is a place in the dark
disconnected from the world,
disconnected from myself.
a place where i am in control,
where i can hurt and punish myself
before anyone else gets the chance.
i search for someone to flip the switch
but fear flips it back off again.
part of me want to break the switch
while jammed in the position of heavy use,
the other part of me wants
to break the switch altogether.
what would happen then?
when you have spent your whole life
living vicariously through others' emotions,
could you even handle
the tsunami wave of emotions unfelt...
or worse yet
find that there was nothing ever there?
is being afraid of my own emotions just a cover up
for something much more sinister?
a locked door to an empty room.
 - *the daughter of a sociopath*

as a child,
you taught me i was bad
through the way
your words and fists hurt me.
you taught me toxic shame
so you could control me
i was helpless.
the only way to survive
was to believe i was as horrible
as the poisonous words
that spewed from your
charmingly wicked mouth.
those words took root in my brain,
a script for my inner critic
a script that ruled my life.
leaving me victim
to lovers like you,
who exploited my caring demeanor
to manipulate my very soul.
for years i have let
all those that i love
rip any shred of confidence
to pieces.
over and over again.

as an adult,
it's time to weed your
poisoned plants from
my mind,
my heart,
my soul.
your words and wounds
are no longer mine to bear.

a child's imagination which saved her
turned into an adult's anxiety
which nearly killed her.
until she discovered the magic was still inside her
she just needed to change the words
to the spells she cast.

broken as a child
i grew older
holding together the
cracked pieces of my soul.
the glue i used to use
no longer worked
and i fell
i fell
   i fell apart
shattering
into a million pieces.

"why do you hate yourself so much?"
when you're taught from a young age
that love means pain and anger...

my heart feels more at home
in the chaos i cause my soul,
for it's all i have ever known.

when i look in the mirror

      i see the devil in my reflection

      .

a child born of trauma,
i learned to hate myself
in order to survive.
now as an adult
i'm trying to learn how to live.
unraveling the seams
of a broken and tattered past.
rewriting my mind in new words
no longer drenched in black and blood
but in light and gold.

{*my trauma is does not define me*}

some days
    my mood swings
        like a child on a swing set
    of an empty playground.

they say
ignorance is bliss.
to live in a world only
as you see it
unwilling to see the world
in ways that don't fit
in the tidy boxes you've designed to feel secure.
how dare you offend me
with your heretic views
for ignorance is safe.
but unfortunately
ignorance is also loud.
    - to all those mean ignorant people

it's hard to be a child
of broken parents,
the damage done by the ones
that were supposed to love them.
it's hard to be a child
of parents who don't know
how to love themselves,
so they show you love
in the only ways they know how.
i was lucky to learn love from my wolf,
unconditional, with no bounds.
i was lucky, that even in a fragmented home
i somehow learned to survive
to see the silver linings,
to learn from my parents' mistakes,
rather than let them consume me
as well.

 - *lessons learned not in vain*

a frightened little girl
resides inside of me
in a dark and hidden cave
obscured from the world.
i keep her deep within the dark
i try my best to keep her safe
but i no longer feel i can,
it seems it's time
            to let the pain in
      .

2 BE A GOOD GIRL

darling,
you'll never see
my heart on my sleeve
i roll them up,
for it's the whole world i deceive.

i paint myself
in all the colors
i pretend to be.

wicked in white
weary old bones
skin that doesn't fit quite right,
the art inside my soul moans.
brimming inside
tormenting to be free
no longer shall you hide
i've listen, i've heard your plea.

some call us nasty
but only because they fear the fire in us
they fear the revolution
they fear losing the privilege
they never even had to fight for.

salted wounds

tell me i look fine,
tell me you'd never know.
i am made of broken pieces
a mosaic of shards
that don't fit quite right
jumbled together and yet
to the rest of the world
i am somehow beautiful,
a beautiful mess.

expectations

expectation
is the death of me.
assumption
persuades my soul.
they walk through my mind
hand in hand
wreaking havoc
everywhere we go.

it's funny how we let
the people we think we love
mold us into something
we are not.
i guess that's how
we should know
for them

               we are not.

when you learn
how to hold yourself together
at a young age
you become a natural.
the world never sees a hint
of how broken you are inside.
no one wants to believe
when you fall to your knees,
shattering everything inside
you have tried to hide,
that you too may need
someone to help.

    someone to help you
stand back up
yet again.

smile,
look pretty,
be good enough,
try harder,
don't show weakness,
be strong,
dress like a girl,
wear makeup,
be feminine,
find a nice boy,
be a good girl,
do as you're told,
be what the worlds expect you to be;
>a well-mannered girl
>looking for a knight in shining armor
>to complete her.
>*- a growling wolf dressed as a princess*

when i was younger,
i was a wild child.
i grew up exploring the wilderness,
my wolf and my imagination
was all i ever needed.
a tomboy,
playing ding dong ditch with the boys
on the houses of pretty girls.
then, i hit puberty first,
suddenly the boys had crushes on me
and the popular girls
wanted to make me one of them.
oh the rumors they told,
the envy,
the endless deceit.
dress me up to look pretty,
but tear me apart from the inside out.
exhausting to live in fear
of constantly having to please others,
no matter what you do,
someone always has something negative to spread.
in the midst of trying to fit in,
i lost myself,
my roots grew weak,
uprooted by trying to mold myself into something
i was not.
left, a hollow girl,
who knew how to look pretty,
but knew nothing of herself.
    - *lost.*

i pried my eyes open
trying to see
what everyone else saw
in me.

cut into my veins
twist and twirl my blood on the floor
until the words drip
"you're pretty"

like a raven
my intelligence is my greatest gift,
yet my worst curse.
i play tricks on my mind
caught in a game with no end,
a problem solver no doubt.
but when the problem has no clever fix
my wings find themselves trapped in the webs,
woven by the spiders that crawl
throughout the crevices of my brain.
gliding through the void,
a bringer of magic and medicine,
in my wake,
i dispel disease of everyone
but myself.
    -the caretaker

i wish water existed
pure enough
to resolve me from myself
cleanse me of my wicked thoughts
curing the darkest parts of me
so when i smile,
it is no longer a mask
for the broken mess
i am inside.

sometimes ugly things
come in beautiful wrapping.

i'm not everyone's cup of tea.
i'm not a floral medley of earl grey,
nor do i bare the soothing essence of jasmine.
i'm not reliable like black tea,
i'm bitter like pine needles.
i'm erratic tasting like that of rose hips.
if you prepare me the wrong way,
i can be quite poisonous like hemlock.
i'm not everyone's cup of tea
but i am,
i am
just me.
searching for a soul who finds me
their warm cup of tea

.

people describe me
as prickly,
abrasive,
as a compliment.
i am who i am.
life has taught me
that pretending to be a person
that makes others feel comfortable
only makes me sicker.
so i may be a porcupine,
but if you deserve it
i'll put down my quills and
let you stroke me.
let you see how soft
i truly am
underneath it all.

i'm sorry i'm not as bad as you thought
or as good as you hoped.

{*the burden of expectations*}

a powerful silence
is found in the
beauty of
        vulnerability.

my hair is wild and free
a semblance of my spirit
that will always remain,
a wolf that can never be tamed.
i'll watch the world crumble at my feet
before a cage i'd ever retreat.

what a feeling
to feel blessed
& cursed
all at the same time.
never knowing which will win,
        the angel or the witch?

it's hard when people say
"you're so strong"
like you ever had a choice.

3 GREY WOLF

in a world of color,
she lives in black and white.
feeling everything
or nothing at all.
a wolf forever grey.

words fail me now
just like my lack of connection,
with myself,
with my emotions.
i float through the day,
as time spins in all directions.
i lay dissociated.
what a peril,
to lose touch with reality,
to lose touch with myself.

hopelessly out reach.

my heart is six feet under
a coffin of my own design
a grave with a hunger
for moonlit eyes.

it's odd,
that rainy days feel gloomy
and the sunshine doesn't feel quite right.
lost somewhere in between.

adrift,
aimlessly,
alone,
empty,
numb,
in a world devoid of color
as life passes by in a daze,
i am not here,
i am disconnected,
hazy eyed
a grey wolf
lost in a world
she no longer belongs to.

the air is bitter,
it fits my twisted soul.
the air is cold,
it matches my frozen heart.
one day i hope spring finds me,
one day i hope spring blooms inside me.

look into my eyes
tell me,
what does your soul see
deep inside of me?

there are no words.
only feelings.

when everything is too much
&
nothing is not enough.

my heart is a masochist.
      & my mind is her enabler.

i'm a hard one to hold,
life has made my heart weary and cold.
i search for in others
what i cannot find within myself,
love.

when the seams come unraveled
but you haven't learned to sew yet.
  - *a seamstress in the making*

i am a supernova
trapped in the ray of light
that creeps between the blinds.

soul binding eyes,
a safe place for others to find.
empathy,
my greatest gift,
my deepest curse.
soul-bound by feeling everything
for everyone else
but nothing for myself.

be careful of the dark my dear,
it's easy to get lost.

gypsy hearted soul &
   heavy hearted lover.

i am cold,
like frozen glass on a winter's eve.
my ash white heart,
like fallen soot from a volcano.
kindle the fire in me once more
find me in the black rocky tundra
devoid of life
wipe the charcoal soot from my eyes
bear fruit
from this rich soil
that goes unsowed.

trapped behind glass eyes
i scream but no one hears my cries.
banging against my skull
a beat i hope spells my demons to a lull.
release me from this hell
help me climb from off this cliff i fell.
so many times i sent out an SOS
but my pleas must not be worth it, i guess.

when it rains
and all the glue
you used
to piece yourself together
comes undone.

i could drown in all my tears

                            unwept.

to be consumed by love
a feeling i crave
yet push away.
i am a twisted tumble weed,
drifting in a desert barren of emotion
hoping to find my oasis in time
time
she has never been on my side.

my soul burns
in cool tone flames
longing
to rekindle my warmth.
    - it has always been up to me.

i feel nothing or everything.
            there is no in between for me.
a black and white lover of all things.

what a funny feeling
to feel as though you walk in the darkness
and it is your shadow that leads the way
forever a passenger
in your own skin
even your shadow knows the way
better than you.

unravel me at me seams,
i dare you to find
what lurks
beneath.

outdated

a vintage grenade
wasting away
in a time i don't belong
well beyond my expiration date
deadly
when everyone thinks i'm harmless
waiting for the shake & rumble
finally pushing my pin out,
nothing left in my wake.
for the moment however,
i sit in wait
just a box full of a junk
gathering cobwebs in the corner
until the day
death blows it all away.

4 SHREDDED BOUNDARIES

purple and blue
the colors of a heart
that has beaten for you
purple and blue
the colors of a heart
beaten by you.

raw

that's how you left me on the floor
raw like the way i mustered the word "No"
how could you hear me over your grunting thrusts.
i left feeling it was my fault,
just like all the bad in my life has always been.
i left with a strange feeling of it all being the same but
different.
when every time you've ever had sex
it feels like rape
what makes actual rape any different than all the rest.
no one has ever heard me say "No" before,
so why should saying those words aloud
make any difference now.

sometimes ugly things
cum in beautiful wrapping.

i was the victim,
but then why do i feel like this was
my fault?

the banquet

darling,
have a taste...
eat your fucking heart out.
because you won't get a piece of mine.
there's nothing left to feast on
in thine hallowed out chest of mine.

did i look pretty unconscious?
while you continued to fuck me,
tears pouring down my face
as i awoke with you inside me,
your hands around my throat.
i can't breathe under the weight of you
as you compressed the
last strength i had out of me
in a muffled scream.
did i look pretty when you left me
naked on the bed
to wash the violence
from your untainted skin.

i guess it makes sense
that i felt you raping me was my fault
that was how i made sense of the way
my father
beat me.
for love is pain
and naturally comes with violence.
are you proud of the girl you raised, dad?

as a child of two alcoholics,
i desire control.
a natural problem solver,
everyone's issue is mine to fix.
a 'save the world' complex.
too bad i never learned
how to save me.

screaming
running
thrown against the wall
pain and anger
fear and shame.
isn't it funny how similar
abuse and rape are,
how one can set us up
to feel we deserved the other.

addicted to your love,
it felt impossible to quit.
i look back now
at all the fucked-up things
you did to me.
how you broke me down
to build yourself up.
  - *love is blind*

do you taste my poetry
when you kiss her lips?

time
will she ever be on my side?

she slept with the light on
so demons wouldn't crawl their way
back into her bed.

what a terrible dance we did
as your body said yes
while mine screamed No
yet your demon's touch still came
filling my secret garden with death
   - *nothing grew there for years.*

i just don't think therapy is helping me.
i know everything they are telling me.
unfortunately,
i just need to do this on my own,
like i always have.
because in the end i'm the only one
who will ever be there for myself.
the only person to help me up
when i fall
because in the end
no one really cares
about anyone but themselves.
        and that's always been the honest truth.

{finding the right type of therapy
  makes all the difference}

what do you do when your own soul
    slips between your fingers,
what do you have to hold on to then?

i don't want to feel you anymore.
if only i could vanquish
the demons you grew in my heart
and in my head.
      i'm not even sure
      an exorcism would do the trick.

i grasp at you like words
to write a poem,
yet you slip
through my fingertips,
for you are not
my poem to hold.

if you're gonna hurt me
why don't i just hurt myself more.

you ruined my hands
drenched in your sin and lie
how can i write
if i no longer
    feel.

they told me to write about you,
i was left empty.
just like how you left me.

how sad it was
that my love was never enough .
how a stranger's gaze
was more enticing to you,
than the bed we shared.

Killed softly by poison laced lips.
As your toxins slowly slipped through my veins.
Your love will always be the deadliest game.

anger
is the emotion one feels
when someone has broken your boundaries.
- the reason we are angry feminists

a wolf
torn to shreds
by human touch,
by human deceit.
a wolf
ripped apart
by those she sought to trust.
ragged fur,
a limping walk,
hollow heart,
only fear and anger remain.
she was once
the queen of the forest,
but now
only her blood red eyes
light the darkness of her cave.

my past
twists and burns my soul.
what is it to live,
when i have only ever known
what it is to survive.

5 A WOUNDED WOLF

tear me to pieces
ravage my mind
release the wolf
inside.

my mind is a demon's playground
what fun they have with me.

trapped in a cage of my own devise
my brain, a cauldron brimming with secrets & lies
this prison i beg to escape
but my mind i do rape
over and over again
there's nothing left for me to defend
what sick games i play with mental health
darling please,
set me free from myself.

i thirst for it.
control.
it's all an illusion.
a false sense of power
that only ever brings us
to our knees.

what words would we find
scribbled in the backside of our mind?

atrophy of crimson and pink
      making space for the horrors i think.

unraveling at the seams
twine spun for stories unknown
twine threaded as life unfolds
tattered edges frayed
as the price of love is paid.

depression is not mine
i do not want it
i do not claim it
but i do share depression with millions.
there is no beauty in my sadness.
your kind words brimming with good intent,
add fuel to my internal wild fire.
    i want to feel what you say about me
but when i look inside me,
all i see is darkness... i want to love myself.
in turn,
i can allow others to love me,
all of me.
not just the pieces i dress up pretty
to make others feel comfortable.
i want to believe
in all the things i know i am.
i want to calm my raging storms,
i want to soothe my beaten soul,
i want to heal me.

in the late hours of the night
when all is quiet and the moon is in sight
my mind races
my heart paces
why is it that i only try to make sense
of all that is in my head
in the hours when it is time for bed?

when i say the words in my head
"i love myself"
it causes me physical pain
nausea in the brain
three words that seem so simple and positive
are words that also show me
i don't know how to live
just yet.

ADHD

organizing the thoughts in my head
is like trying to find a pattern
in a pan full of scrambled eggs.

{what a mess}

what it's like to live in a world
without a filter,
to find importance
when every stimuli
is given equal priority,
you sit there
overwhelmed
and misunderstood,
as if the meds
truly made much of a difference.

i have so much pain inside me
it wells up
spilling out the corners of my eyes,
the salt burns the scars from years past
i hold my breath.
this too will pass,
i hope.
i hope that the light in the distance never goes out.
somedays it's harder to see than others
but i know
deep down inside it's still there.
sometimes it flickers,
as i grasp out to hold its ember
blowing on it to reignite its once bright flames.
it escapes my hands,
ever left in the darkness,
chasing my lightning bug on a muggy summer night.
will your warmth ever melt my frozen hands,
filled with black blood,
from a heart that struggles to muster a beat,
to find a rhythm that i can once again dance to.
how can i explain my body
in this catatonic state?
frozen in fear of things that don't exist.
i fear to move for most days
i do not trust my wicked hands,
for they have found their way
to false lovers, pills, and sharp blades.
so i lay here in silence
staring at the cold white ceiling
i dare not move,
shallowly breathing,
i hold my breath
this too will pass
i hope.

slit my wrist and
save me from myself.

protect me,
from the monsters
that hide in my head
and beneath my bed.

they told me sticks and stones
will break my bones.
they never told me,
i'd be the one
who wields them.
they never told me,
they'd be
my mind's weapons of choice.

i'm sorry
i'm sorry for everything.
i'm sorry for me.
i'm sorry.
i am
so sorry.

    {toxic guilt}

a fickle thing
to listen to your heart
& your mind,
fearing who's right.

when our mind goes silent,
is that when we finally fall apart,
as the pieces crumble
from too many attempts
of putting them back
or
is that when all the pieces
finally fall together
and become one.

a heart so passionate
a heart so broken
holding on to things i shouldn't
holding on to things that hurt me
do i do it because i hate myself?
do i do it to punish myself?
or do it because it keeps me safe
from letting anyone else in?
perhaps,
a toxic cocktail of it all.

why do we love all the wrong people?

{*asking for a friend*}

toxic people,
pray on those
who are kind and care for others.
they tear you to pieces,
in backhanded compliments,
little ways they phrase things,
to rip at damaged parts of your heart.
they make you think they love you,
but file your soul down so small,
that their version of you
is all you feel you have left.
they do this to control you.
when you point out the red flags,
they make it seem like you're crazy
and somehow it's all your fault.
toxic relationships
can NOT be maintained.
if you let weeds into your garden,
they will take over,
no matter what you do.
so take things slow,
it's worth the wait,
to give the key
to your secret garden,
to the one who is willing
to help you tend it.

let it go,
i whisper to myself.
let it go.
my heart strains as the
words tumble from my quivering lips.
it hurts to hold on to you,
it hurts more to let you go.
so i fill myself to the brim
with toxic shame.
a cauldron,
bubbling over.
as i burn myself
from the inside out.

  {*holding on to acid*}

thoughts swirl in my mind
i repeat to myself
"you can only control yourself"
i can observe my thoughts,
therefore, they are not me.
yet it feels the only thing
i can't control
is myself.

the wheels turn inside my head
they seem to understand
all that's wrong inside of me
yet my heart still frozen,
refuses to accept.

my mind is a terrifying thing.
racing thoughts slowly eat away
at all of me.
never knowing what horrors
tomorrow will bring.
i lay crippled
by monsters that refuse to cease.
i crave to be set free
but i never find release.
relentlessly caged in a circle of traps
created by my own mental design.
darkness consuming my glimmer of hope,
as i resist sealing my fate
on the dotted line.
i bear down,
scrambling to cope.
"i'm so fucked up in the head"
tormented by demons,
until one of us is dead.

wood bowed from
tear soaked panels
of the bedroom floor.

blackness seeps into my mind
crumbling barriers,
nothingness is all that's left behind.
a disorder,
a disease,
a plague.
tendrils leech through the veins of my skull,
no part of me shall survive the cull.

taking over
losing control
too late for white flags
too late for hope.

my armor corroded by the venom,
no vaccine to save me now.

i have what i like to call 'broken bird' syndrome
i like to date broken birds
maybe if i heal them
or make them feel a little bit better
as brief as it may be
i will feel better
perhaps even accomplished
maybe even heal myself in the process
however the broken bird
that needs the most healing
is me
but i do not accept that
because it's far too hard
so instead
my therapist replies
"have you ever dated someone with their shit together?"

do you ever think i can learn to love,
do you ever think i can learn to love myself?

it hurts to talk sometimes.
the pain seems to boil in my veins,
welling up inside me,
slipping out in tears that roll down my rosy cheeks.
contrasted by lack of color in the rest of my skin.
i am falling,
ever waiting to hit the ground,
as all of me spills out on the floor.
maybe then the pain that has been
carved into my bones
will finally cease,
as they shatter to white dust.
i crave peace from this internal war,
a weary soldier who has fought for too long,
i crave solace from this battle i have raged
against myself.
to let me fall.
falling
     f
   a
    l
    l
     i
      n
      g
       fall.

cutting

a self-loathing form of cathartic release,
to feel anything
to feel in control of the pain.
the pain you feel so out of your control.
to be released from the mind-numbing
nothingness that devours your soul.
so numb, so detached,
as you run from your pain
you contemplate if you even truly exist.
the rush of pain,
the crimson unveiling,
reminds me i can still feel
reminds me i am alive
reminds me i am real.

                                        nowadays
                    i have found healthier ways to cope
                            it's hard to resist the urge,
                    when you feel you have no choice,
                                        oh but you do.
                        love and joy will find you,
                    if you open your soul to them
                            relinquish your fear
                            of holding onto things
                                you must let go.
                    this false sense of control
                            only keeps us stuck,
                        we must accept pain,
                            it is a part of life
                                but suffering
                        is a choice we make.

it helps to write
to release what's inside
putting ink to paper
instead of blade to wrist.
violently they twist
i press down harder
emotions pour,
releasing the flooded tide inside
my storming mind
brimming with words redefined
violently they twirl
as healing force unfurls
my hand dances to prose unread
my darkness born of beauty instead
the words may not turn scarlet red
but their onyx pitch against moonlit white,
reminds me to see
in the darkness there is always light
in the darkness of night,
the wolf shall always find her fight.

the whispers
from the darkest parts of my mind
are quiet now.
8 days, 8 days,
i have resided in the walls
of this psychiatric hospital.
i have learned new ways
to keep my demons at bay,
repetitive lullabies
to rest their eyes.
perhaps what brings me most strength
is to know
i am not alone
i am not alone in this battle,
that people from all walks of life
stumble and fall,
with scraped knees and cuts that bleed,
we help one another stand on our feet
as we fight our demons down to defeat.

hopelessly i cry
in clouds high up in the sky
i beg for the words in my head to stop
hiding from the world, running out the clock.
trapped inside my mind
by the demons that reside
no longer in control
release me to decide
like a phoenix i will rise.

nightmares
my old friends
they keep me company through the night
what horrors lay inside my mind's darkest theme
they make me cry and scream
with such a fright
they wonder how i function on such little sleep
it's easy when you're terrified
of what your mind will reap.
so i sleep with the lights on
not in fear of the monsters
that hide under my bed
but the more dreadful ones
that lurk in my head.

on rainy days
the ink on my page runs
making way for a
black nothingness of numb
forever raining

sew my lips shut
perhaps then i'll finally be safe
from love that isn't real
from things i wish not to feel

where do my emotions go
when i do not feel
when i am numb to the world
how is it that when i feel
it's a flood of all i refuse to accept
and when i do want to feel
it seems as though there is nothing beneath the seal.

{emotions are always there}

what a terrible feeling
to hold yourself hostage
for you cannot trust
even your own hands
with the sanctity of your life.

{a promise to fight depression}

i broke myself into pieces
trying to patch the broken parts of you.
i wasn't left with much when you left.
in the darkness
i found self-love,
gleaming like afternoon sun rays
that creep through cracked blinds.
yet in me,
it poured from gaping holes.
every day the light reminds me
to be kind & gentle
with myself.
that it's okay to put myself first
that i am worthy
of love from others &
especially myself.

anxiety is fear.
fear of the unknown
fear of no control
fear of the things
that pile up on your chest.
breathless they grow
like monsters
i pretend don't
hide under my bed
i pretend
don't hide
in my head
eating away at pieces of me
until it feels there's nothing left
i collect the scraps of me
mustering on
not sure
if i am hoping for it all to end
or for tomorrow to be a better day...
    - *will it ever get better?*

my heart swells,
as the ocean does,
do you think she cries as i do?

ptsd is so hard
we have so much fear
feeding our inner critic,
we destroy ourselves
so it hurts less
when others hurt us.
we survive
but in doing so
we forget how to live.

i try to run from things
i can never escape
till my feet slip
on their own blood,
drowning in the spilt pool
of my own undoing.

salt crystals
lay upon my pillowcase
formed from tears
that sneak from my eyes at night
while i lay trapped in nightmares of you
and all the other demons i've faced
and have yet to conquer.

{*warriors cry too*}

you changed me,
my heart cast in iron
my mind fragile as porcelain.

just another name for anxiety

when becoming numb
is the only way to survive
we crave to feel alive
but when we do feel
we drown in everything unfelt
and just like that
the fear
switches it all off
again.
~~fear is my greatest enemy~~

depression.

    being sad
    when you have nothing
    to be sad about,
        & feeling horribly guilty about it.

self-sabotage
is the game,

checkmate.

the keys of her typewriter lay rusted
from the tears of her self-loathing.

{*a howling wolf*}

i am
the master
of my own
demise.

i want to be the one who saves myself
from this quicksand
i'm sinking in.
why can't i?
yanked from the path
of making my dreams come true,
i still see where i want to be
just out of reach.
if only my arms were a little longer
perhaps then
i could grasp my glimmer of light,
pulling myself from this muck.
or perhaps,
i am forever stuck.

6 UNLOCKING THE CLOSET DOOR

the wrong fit

i never felt quite right
as i tried to entertain
the conventional notion of falling in love
with who the world saw fit as natural.
a broken girl
of a broken father
was always my excuse
as they say
"daddy issues"
i tried all different types
but they never did fit right…

blooming out of the closet

in a new city
i had the chance to
discover me
free from the shackled version
that sat comfortably in other peoples
perceptions' of me.
people prefer when you fit in the nice tidy box
they have made for you.
but in a new city
i had no box to hide in,
just my raw soul
to discover.

butterflies

for the first time
i met someone
who gave me goose bumps
who made me nervous
who made my cheeks blush rosy pink
she gave me feelings
i had never felt before
a funny delightful feeling
that gave my soul wings
& fluttered inside of me

she took off my clothes
kissing parts of me
awakening my soul
igniting my skin
with her passionate touch.
bliss,
is what she gave me
as my legs quivered
around her midnight kiss.

    - the moment i knew i was gay

finally sex
wasn't just something
that happened to me.
it was magic
we shared
with one another
lying together as
one.

i remember
how terrified i was
the first time it was my turn
to reciprocate the ecstasy
i was intimately given.
i felt like a virgin, a novice,
a million thoughts raced through my mind.
but as my lips met
the ones unveiled between her legs,
i was consumed in that moment
for all i cared about was
her.

gender

gender is here nor there.
how could they ever presume
two words
would be enough to describe a world of us.
each person unique from the next
we will never be confined by our sex.
so my darling,
i'll give you some advice.
now listen closely,
being something you're not
will never suffice... be unequivocally You,
because that is beauty.
be unequivocally You,
because that is unapologetically
who You are.

androgyny is about
the simultaneous existence of
both masculinity and femininity.
people's concept of "androgyny"
involving only a masculine-presenting person
devalues the very existence of femininity.
i believe in existing somewhere outside
the gender binary,
where all facets of who i am
can be appreciated,
rather than denied.

i choose the feminine pronoun
not because it describes me
there is no pronoun in existence that describes me
to use the plural implies my identity is unknow
which denies my exact interwoven concept of self.
i use the female pronoun,
honestly,
because it sounds pretty.
the way the lips and
the tongue dance
as you pronounce
"she"
just as you taste
the most feminine
parts of me.
i want to live in
a world that isn't
described in black and white,
where we can all exist
in the rainbow in between.

i didn't know i was gay from the age of a child,
my crushes on girls & boys
never made much sense at that age,
nothing really did,
the world still had so much
for me to discover.
when i did come out,
it was funny looking back,
       as they say hindsight is 20/20.

    (i wish my vision was too)

it takes courage to be
who you want to be
and not to be the person
others want you to be.
it's okay not to be visible,
we celebrate you too.
your identity is real.
your identity is valid.
it took me time to accept
the fact that being female
did not fit my gender identity.
gender is a spectrum,
it's not something that fits in a neat tidy box,
it is not blue or pink.
it's anything you want it to be!
there are beautiful aspects of me
that are both
masculine & feminine.
my identity is in harmony,
it is balanced,
some days it sways one way more than the other.
that doesn't mean my identity changes on a daily basis
but i am fluid with how i choose to present it.
gender identity and presentation
are two separate things.
they can match or they may not.
to this day i am still working
on feeling comfortable in my own skin,
uncovering what feels right for me.
most importantly, learning to love myself.
now, i don't let the opinions of others define me.
i am me, whether anyone else cares or not,
doesn't matter
as long as i am happy
with who i am.

be you,
be proud,
don't let anyone
tear you down.
for you are the color
that lights this world.
in your unique radiance,
you create space for
the beauty
of life itself.

when i was little,
i was different.
i was a wild and weird tomboy,
who played rough on the playground
and shopped in the little boy's section.
in elementary school,
i was beat up and bullied;
called a dyke, gay, a rug muncher among other things.
i remember thinking to myself,
"i am happy and colorful
(the definition for gay i found in the dictionary)
but who eats rugs!?"
i was too young to understand
what the girls who bullied me
already knew.
i spent a long time thinking
i was broken when it came to relationships,
accepting the realization that
i would spend the rest of my life
alone.
when i moved to new orleans,
i found a city that celebrated differences,
free to discover myself hidden
beneath years of suppression;
things i resisted but knew for quite some time.
i have never been happier
with who i am as a person
now that i no longer have to hide
who i am
from myself.
after experiencing my first true heartbreak
and how awful it truly is,
i still wouldn't trade any of it,
to go back to feeling
nothing at all.
i'm so lucky i have such amazing friends and family.
i remember being afraid to come out to my family.
i had survived relatively unscathed
from all the adversity i had overcome
but if i was gay

somehow,
that would make more sense to others,
that i did end up messed up and broken from
everything i went through.
luckily, my family was accepting,
some even said they were wondering
when i was going to figure it out.
at the end of the day,
coming out to myself
was the hardest challenge of it all.
i am so grateful to be uniquely me,
and all that encompasses.
so darling please,
don't ever fear what makes you different,
accept what makes you
all that you are.

{you will always be beautiful to me}

the scars we bare,
tell a story of pain.
that we are still alive-
tells a story of triumph.
your beauty is for the world to see
even if they don't see it yet.
smile,
one day they will.

many people wonder
how they know they are queer.
it's not about just having an experience
to figure it out.
when you find someone
who is special,
who you connect with,
it will be a meaningful experience,
no matter their biological sex or gender identity.
it's about being open to connection
with what's in someone's heart,
not between their legs.
find the person
whose heart resonates with yours,
find a safe place to explore love
and determine what love means to you.
coming out to Yourself
is truly the hardest part.

there is no timetable to come out,
it's okay to take the time you need,
there is no rush, no paperwork,
it's your decision.
when you are ready,
you will know.
remember always to be safe and
have a good support network
to help you in this journey.
coming out is about you,
no one else.
when you do come out,
shine.
be you,
uniquely you,
explore the parts of yourself
you didn't dare before.
in opening this door,
you have the opportunity
to love yourself completely.

"you're too pretty to be gay"
this notion burns me to my core
i feel the fury boiling up inside my veins
a tempest ripe to sink his soul.
i inhale slow and deep,
i exhale letting my muscle relax
as each ml of torrid air escapes my lungs.
his ignorant words only show
the limits of a small insecure mind.
i settle for a cheeky response,
"what does that even mean?"
and with a smile i walk away
as the pompous man is left stupefied
by a question that
never even crossed his mind.

why is my sexuality
always up for debate,
simply because i am not straight?
No,
no boy broke my heart,
i broke theirs.
No,
i have met many amazing men,
but i could never love them
like they loved me.
No,
i have been fucked right,
by a woman.
No,
you can't turn me straight,
my sexuality is not a switch
you can flip for your delight.
No,
i don't want to have a three way,
and No,
you cannot watch my girlfriend and i have sex.
why comments like these
are seen as socially acceptable
horrifies me,
it makes me angry
it makes me want to hide from the world,
it makes me loath society.
me and my sexuality
are not here for you to fetishize.
i am human,
my sexuality is valid,
my love is real.
you don't have the right
to reduce me to a degraded fantasy.
i don't deserve to be treated this way
just because of
who i choose to love.

sexuality is fluid.
just like gender identity and expression.
we like things to be fixed,
because it's natural to fear change,
we fear the unknown.
it's okay not to know
everything about yourself.
it's okay to change yourself,
in doing so,
you may just discover a bit more
of who you truly are.

homosexuality is not unnatural,
many species of life display love in this way.
love is love, oh and it is beautiful.
do not be afraid to love who you love,
do not let the fear of others dictate your life,
explore your world, your heart, your soul,
and everything it has to offer.

"oh, i wish i could be gay"
speaking from experience,
being gay is not easier than being straight,
in fact, it is much harder.
if i had the choice, i would be straight,
it's easier, you don't have to love in fear.
but it took me a long time to discover
that holding a woman's heart
is what makes me happy.
although it is not easier,
it is love,
and i wouldn't trade it for the world.

don't let the world fool you
into loving the way society wants.
don't let naive people
teach you that your love is wrong.
don't you dare let the world
keep you from finding a heart to call home.
   - *your love is valid, love on.*

i spent so much of my life,
trying to hide the wolf inside,
trying to fit in,
amongst sheep.
it took me a long time
to discover me,
to discover the love
of a she wolf
is the love for me.

,

7 ALONE WOLF

she preferred to be alone
to sit quietly with her demons,
even though she knew
the lone wolf
never survives.

they say misery loves company,
mine seems to love none.

a black sticky mess
don't you dare fall in love
with this black tar heart of mine
for darling,
my darkness is a death trap
that no one sees.

for me,
liking someone
is like getting into a cold pool.
i'm likely to only dip my toe in
deciding it's not worth the jump.
not worth
letting my body assimilate
to a new temperature.
so i play it safe
forever sitting on the side lines,
forever sitting poolside.

i'm bad at love
a love like poison.
the midas touch
where everything
i touch
is ruined.

an alchemist
drink my potion
consume my bewitching love.
slowly my dark magic
seeps into your blood,
hexing words
creep into your mind,
i will destroy you
like all the rest.

heart block.

like a lightning bolt to my heart
an arrhythmia you did start.
now i struggle correcting this distorted beat,
there's nothing left after your endless deceit.
   - *to my ex-lover*

cupid's embrace.

she traced the outline of my cupid bow lips,
dripping with honey were her seductive finger tips.
a demon dressed in angel wings,
spellbound as the siren sings.
my ship crashed into her rocky shore,
i should have seen the blood drenched waves,
i should have listened to the lore.

cardio.

they ask me how i stay so skinny;
i spend all day running,
from myself,
from my past,
from my present,
from my future.
i spend all day running from these demons,
despite my every repent.
when you feel wicked to the bone,
there is no escape.
so i run fast & oh so alone.
     [time traveler on the run]

the moon

have you ever howled to the moon,
her cold pale skin against the dark horizon
as awake she did soon.
jealous every evening of how she dances with the sun.

have you ever seen her smile,
watched each night as her heart grew brighter
watching her bloom, enchanting, & beguiled
falling in love with her as the night grew quieter

have you ever loved the moon,
bled against rough edges of her scars
promised yourself to let her go
seeing her darkness amongst the stars
but your love for her never ceased to glow

have you ever howled for the moon,
begged her to listen to your song
only to love her more by daybreak
oh for her how you longed
but you were only ever left with heartache.

she hasn't left yet,
then why does it feel like
she already has?

a black rose
watered by the tears
of a broken heart.

my porcelain heart
has lost many of its pieces
not much remains
to even break.
and if you shatter what's left,
nothing more will ever exist.

a hollow chest
an empty soul.
an eerie echo of a heartbeat.
so like a feral wolf
alone
i guard what's left.
instead of howl,
i snarl at the stars
who call to me.
i'm safer,
alone.

when all my love stories
surmount to a body count.
darling you'll see,
i will bring you begging to your knees.
feel my hand wrapped around your throat,
heart tense,
my love is a sealed death sentence.

abandonment issues

to taste your lips
a future lover
as i wrap my arms around your hips
full of lust and wonder
let's create magic
you and me
a heartbreak undoubtedly tragic
but perhaps we'll see
if you're the girl who finds the key
maybe just this once
you'll stay forever here with me.

my wicked heart
locked deep within
a maze of tragic gardens.
only black roses grow,
thorns covered in blood.
oh,
and the walls my dear,
drenched in venom,
laced with poison.
no one dares to seek what lurks inside,
for only the creatures of darkness here reside.

a double-edged sword.
she was my poetic love
enchanted
the words poured from my mouth
warming the deepest anchors of my soul.
lonely
as she left
the words still came
bleeding from my dead cold finger tips.

she gave me roses drenched in black
ripped from my garden
she once bloomed in my heart
and just like that
the plague rotted all that grew there.
brittle bones crumble
in the wake of her storm
which once, captivated my soul.
all too soon,
only the dust of me remained.

my love for you
runs deep
even after all you've done
i still find myself missing you
but i will never take you back.
our battle is over.
but i will continue
to weed you from my garden,
until i am free of you
until my dying breath.

what a surreal feeling
to miss someone
you haven't even met.

kiss me,
drown
in my poetry.

a beautiful rose
i held you too tightly
pierced by your thorns
my wild lupine heart loved too brightly
i fell, tangled in your vine
forever my
bloody valentine.

she was beautiful
in the way she lied
and i hung myself on every word
as if they were true.
   {*the noose around my neck*}

icarus and her sun

i craved passionate love
one which ignited fires in my soul
bringing spring's sweet relief
to my icy heart
naive
i didn't think to fear the burn
a love forged in flames
would leave in its wake.
for fire can only burn for so long
in one place.
~~there's nothing left~~

no matter what i could have done,
it wouldn't make a difference.
far too many sleepless nights
i spent searching,
searching,
for that one little detail to rewrite,
the one that could change our storyline.
imagining a version
where i could have saved us
and all the magic we once were.
the truth is,
nothing could change our forsaken finale.
for long before me,
you sold your soul to the devil.
a blood oath,
not even angel's blood could unbind.

a serpent's kiss
you whispered sweet spells into my ear
with your snake like demon tongue
slithering your grasp tighter around my soul
you made me fall in love with a person that wasn't real
constricting tighter and tighter,
filling my heart with false love
i thought it was butterflies you gave me,
i found out,
they were only ever moths.
you promised to be my forever
little did i know
it was all a well-conceived trap.
your insecurities wreaked havoc on my mind,
molding me
into your little marionette doll.
beguiled by your charm and wit
constricting tighter and tighter,
a vice around my heart
mesmerized by your love
i didn't dare fight back
blinded by the venom
you spit in my eyes
consumed by your intoxicating rapture,
i sat helpless
as i watched you devour my heart
till there was nothing left.
till there was nothing left of me.
and you left me there.
a hollow ghost
of a once bright and whimsical girl.

now,
i drift aimlessly through this grey world,
you took all the color with you,
my heart simply wasn't enough
for your glutinous ways
you slithered away with all of the parts of me
i loved
about myself.

left only with your black and poisonesssss love.
it seeps through my pores,
running rampant through my veins
my neurons burn
in the flames of your deceitful wake.

i have yet to find the antidote,
i'm not sure one exists
for an alchemy like yours.
your love is pain
just like all the love i have ever known.
it burns
& it aches
you think i would have seen the signs
after the way
my father taught me
love was black and blue,
oh but you knew how to fill my world with magic
before you burnt it all down to ashes.

so i sit here
missing you
despite all you've done
wondering
if the devil could truly be
my soulmate.
i sit here wondering
what i could have done different,
feeling like somehow
your tongue
between another girl's legs
was my fault.
remembering all the good
while all the bad slinks away into
the dark corners of my mind,
hidden & hazily forgotten.

i fight myself every day;
i want to be with you,
we could fix this...

no.
we can never fix this.
would being with you fix me, are you all i deserve?
deep down in the storming seas of my soul,
i know i deserve better.
your sea serpent ways
show no semblance of remorse,
& somehow you made me
the villain.
i want to fix the mess you've made of me.
but how can i fix this broken heart
when you didn't even leave me
the pieces?

i was a candle
her love the flame
her warmth a facade
she burnt me till my wick's end
i was left
a puddle
on a dark and dusty shelf
turned cold and hard
yet fragile and
spread far too thin.

gone
is the melancholy prose
that filled my pages
and drenched my soul.

8 MOONLIT LOVERS

the moon is mine
as i am hers.

drawn to ladies who drenched their skin
in the light of the midnight moon
pure & surrounded by darkness
let us drink our sins
like a glass of red wine.

galaxies exist in your sapphire eyes
enchanted by your lustful stare
you awaken parts of me
hidden within dark
casting shadows away
with your seductive touch
i quiver
i shake
as i whisper
your name in your ear
universes collide
the rush.
my body moans for your kiss.
bring me to my knees
your eyes will be
my sweetest demise.

her skin was pure
like freshly fallen snow
oh, but her touch
awoken the coldest parts
of my soul.

awaken this dusty porcelain heart of mine
sitting wearily in the corner china cabinet.
pick the lock on the cupboard door,
what treasures you may find.
gently cup me in your hand's duet
revive me with your heaven's kiss.
as you softly feel the pitter patter bliss
of my heart's surrendered beat amiss.

i want the kind of love
that makes poetry bleed gold
from my fingertips.

a–muse me

she inspires me
my muse of bliss
as words drip down my fingertips
stumbling over the enigmatic rhythm, you siren.

that smile

that smile of hers
captivates my soul
lost in her beautiful darkness
seduced by spellbinding emerald eyes
oh
but when she laughs
not even my demons
have a place to hide.

you are not easy to read my dear
i long for the day
the pages of your book
become well worn
by my fingertips,
as i've read all your lines a thousand times
and discovered
all that is hidden between.

kiss my lips
watch me tremble
beneath your hips.

your sweet nectar drips down my face
how i crave to be drenched in your gold.

enamored
her love
turned me
progressively
more sappy
until i became
maple syrup
in her hands.

swallowing her
like smooth liquor
intoxicating my heart
to beat and flutter.
it breaks my ribs
only to be closer
to her
melting me like warm butter.
i'd gladly sink
to the darkest depths
of her storming seas.

bloom flowers in my heart.

stay close to my heart always.
you light the stars in my soul,
the neurons in my brain,
you feel like drops of sinful bliss on my skin.
you make the world stop
and spin
all at the same time.
it's as if you make
the sun rise,
in a world of darkness.
it's as if you are the full moon shining bright
when there is nothing more to light the way.
you ignite my soul with blue flames.
they burn small and slow
but all consuming.
as your skin touches mine,
no symphony could compare.
as your heart beats close to mine,
it beats harder,
in hopes to only beat
a little bit closer to yours.
when we lay bare in bed,
your body against mine,
i feel multiple universes
melt into one
as we become one.
you, my love, are everlasting.

when i think of you
gold ink spills across my page
filling me up with words
i can't compose the lyrics to
you make my heart sing.

she awoke
with star dust flickering
from her sleepy eyes
in this vulnerable moment,
she looked up at me,
"do you still love me today?"
she mumbled.
with a soft kiss
on her forehead
i replied,
"i still love you today.
tomorrow.
and every day after that."

i want to be the girl
who turns your beauty
into poetry
as your heart falls
for my every word,
i promise to always
catch her in my hands.

walk with me in smoke and ember.
darling, take my hand
& be my anchor.

my flame.
her smile ignites my lunar eclipse.

she is wildfire.
mesmerizing and dangerous.
in her wake she only leaves
blackness and death.
witness her beauty from afar
but don't get entrapped in her dance,
too close
and all that will remain
is ashes.

whisper me your misery
whisper me your dark desires
let me lift the veil
let me light this love on fire
may it never dim
like the flicker of light
i see in your soul
like the flicker of light
that draws me into your darkness.

{a moth to a flame}

speak to me in tongues
of other worldly realms
as my hands grab your waist
you can't escape my gravitational pull
let our worlds collide
ignite
burn infinity in between.
phoenix love,
let us rise from the ashes
as one.

{lovers under the full blood moon}

the electrons race between
our skin's embrace.
this my dear is chemistry,
your solution is me.

i feel her thunder through my veins
a lightning storm my heart sustains.

she is the ocean.
i am the shore.
every day i build sand castle walls
around this wounded heart,
with every change of the tides
she tumbles them down.
teaching me what it is to be vulnerable again.
for i am her apprentice,
as we crash into one another
guiding me to dance
in her ebb and flow.
perhaps one day
i'll let her healing waters
sail my heart away
on the curves of her waves
perhaps i let her teach me
what love truly is.

    - to the girl i've yet to meet

you touch me
sticky & wet
like warm maple syrup
what a beautiful mess we make
entwined embrace
dancing bodies in bed
drops of sweet sugar drip
on my tongue and fingertips.

my mouth waters at the taste
of your succulent flower
let your poison hypnotize me
as i watch your rhythmic dance beneath me
let your hidden thorns drain me of all that i am
eaten up by your deviant intoxication
i come undone for you.

blood moon magic.

ink drips down my finger tips
like blood from freshly slit wrists.
kiss me with your scarlet lips
sink with me into the veil,
the darkness insists.
feel my withered heart crumble in your palms
let this crimson magic quiet your demoness qualms.

i want to get lost
between your legs
find the darkest corners
of your soul
the ones you didn't even know
existed.
that's where i'll bloom my garden
that's where i'll feed you,
until you're brimming
with my love.

you my love
have fermented in my soul
grown roots
in cracks of my frozen frail bones.

i wish i was falling asleep
to the pitter patter of your heart beat
as my earth moves and quakes
with the rise and fall
of each breath you take

endlessly looking
for that poetic love

i want to exist with you
in the spaces between
the lines of my poetry
the place where
magic still exists.

i want to sample your heart beat
as we move to rhythm &
synchronize to the base line

my galaxy
  unravel me at my seams
  darling please,
  undress me.
  fire flickers in your eyes,
  raging.
  as i slip my fingers down the curve
  of your porcelain skin.
  quiver and shake beneath me
  as your soul reaches out
  pulling mine to yours
  we are one
  floating through galaxies
  we never dreamed existed
  but you
  my dear
  are real
  the sparks between us
  only kindle our flames
  as we devour one another.

moonlit skin
turquoise eyes
awaken me with you midnight howl
bones to dust
ignite the stars that flicker in your eyes
kiss me with lips made of gold
my darling,
make me unfold.

stay.

unexpected
you tip-toed into my life
with a force that consumed me
when you finally revealed yourself
you became even more beautiful in my eyes.
real, rough, with pieces of you still scattered
and a simple awkward smile that lit up my world.
                    what storms we have braved, my darling.
                    you slipped into my veins, intoxicating me,
                    until my lungs filled with your sweet words
                            leaving me breathless.
                    you enveloped my heart in gold
                        sealing it with a nervous kiss
                            in a busy train station
                    that seemed empty once our eyes met
                                    so stay
                    though you may shake and tremble
                                    stay
                        and let me love you
                        for the rest of forever.

                    {*i begged but she had already left*}

sinful bliss
that's what i found
in her whirlpool eyes
of shimmering turquoise
the thought of her lips against mine
and i'm soaring
on the tips of iridescent raven wings.

i want to sip the dandelion milk
that spills from between you
as it cleanses my wicked hands.

you didn't just bloom a garden in my heart
you made way for an entire forest.

i sipped your moonlit smile
one taste is all it took
for me to drown.

your skin is red wine on my lips
drench me in your sin.

kindle the dimming stars
in my midnight moon heart.

i want to be alone,
alone with you.
i long to kidnap
your fragile heart
& hold you safe
locked away
in my treasure chest.

{a wolf in shining armor}

take my hand,
get lost with me in this dark land.
what wicked delights
you will unveil
in thirst of my wolf like bite.

you are beautiful
in the most unique
and magical of ways.
you are not defined
by traditional beauty.
the beauty of your soul
is not bound by skin and bones,
it gleams beyond the limits of others.
the whole world gets a glimpse
of your unexposed allure.
however, only a few
have been blessed with
your fragile glowing brilliance,
the face behind
your well-designed mask.

unveil my infinite radiance,
witness the intertwined dark roots grown
from surviving what most, would not.
i, my dear, will show you what no other could.
i will show you how rare you truly are.
you are more than a work of art,
you are more than a masterpiece,
you are once in a life time.
a gem from beyond this realm.
a summation of all that you have endured,
finding resilience where no one else could
    - inside of you.
you, my love,
     are a magnum opus.

i know you are tired my dear
i know you have fought
for more years than a young girl should
i know the outside world scares you
from all the harm it has caused you.
i know the mirrors have a wicked way
of showing you things that are unreal,
but i promise, they only deceive you.
i know that human connection is hard for you
which only makes it harder to connect with yourself,
especially when you feel you can't hold on.
i know at times
your body finds it difficult to hold on to your soul.
i know you have a beautifully fragile strength about you
& a body frail from abuse at length.
but know that i am here.
rest your tired eyes and
brittle bones against my chest.
let the beat of my heart be your calming lullaby
that lays your head to rest.
when you are afraid &
your soul leaps from its earthly bounds,
see that i am right here to hold your hand,
until you find your way home again.

and suddenly
our breath became one
as our heartbeats
synchronized to the
same harmony.
finally,
i found you.

the stars could never dream of
shining as bright as she does
when she smiles.

bloom flowers in my heart
the kind that grow wild
right into my soul
let their petals spread out
basking in your warm light
let me feel your love in every single vein of me
as they spread throughout my bones
and when winter's first snow comes
let the dust of them remain
sparkling on my skin
like your moonlight kisses
i hope you're still there to give
stay a while
with me
let us blossom
a perennial effervescent garden
a love that lasts forever
blooming each year
more than the last.

my love,
thank you for understanding me
when no one else could.
thank you for knowing how difficult emotions
can be for me, for the both of us.
thank you for making me not feel so lost
& holding my hand through the darkness
when i couldn't find my way.
thank you for believing in me
when i couldn't believe in myself.
thank you for making me smile when i felt i forgot how.
thank you for constantly helping me to be patient with
all life hands me, but most of all,
being patient with myself.
thank you for reminding me that the compassion i give
to others, i must also give to myself.
thank you for finding beauty in all
the cracked pieces of me, as i put them back together.
thank you for inspiring me to write,
to be creative, challenging me to allow myself
to be in touch with my emotions.
thank you for calling me out on my irrational bullshit
when i have trouble turning my self-critic off.
thank you for pushing yourself to be the person you
want to be, even when it seems like an impossible feat.
thank you for making all the bad melt away,
even if it's just for a moment.
thank you so incredibly much
for holding on to hope for me when i no longer could.
thank you for forgiving me
for things i struggle to forgive in myself.
thank you for staying, despite our tendency to run,
you have stayed through so much more bad than good.
thank you for teaching me that not only can i be loved,
i deserve love.
this last one is most important...
thank you for being You.

i was a rabid wolf,
trying to learn to control
the wild inside
the wild that allowed me to survive.
you reached out to me
your heart in your hand
you trusted me not to devour it whole
even as i snarled as you tiptoed closer to me
you showed me kindness and love
like no one ever had
i now lay tamed,
in your arm's embrace.
you accepted my wild,
inspiring me to live
to love,
not only you, but
to love myself.
you soothe my aching soul
with your patient touch,
a gift i can never repay
but will spend every day trying
to love you in all the wild ways
you deserve.

9 LEARNING TO HOWL

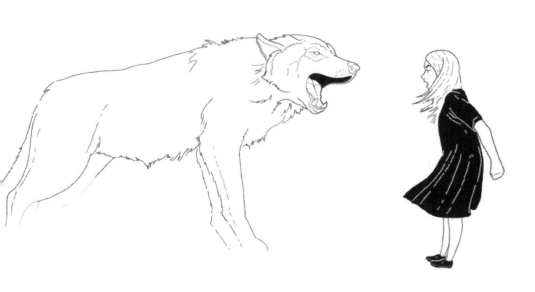

my soul sits
undecided in what feels
like comfort.
the healing process has left me...
without a place that feels right.
perhaps tomorrow,
she'll decide.

the breaking

through the cracks in our souls
especially the ones that break
beyond our control
within them
we truly find ourselves
we finally get to read
the book with
the worn binding
the one on the shelf
that always seemed out of reach.

some days there are glimpses of hope,
the dust filled rays glimmer through
the cracked wooden panels of my mind.
on these days i return light's grace with a smile,
and for a moment there's peace,
in my blood-stained mind.

maybe my rough and jagged edges
just need a little sanding
for the light to shine through.

{*a diamond in the rough*}

and some days an elephant takes up residence
on my chest.
those days
what a struggle it is to move
eventually running
through the maze work of my mind,
i find some peanuts to throw
and the weight is lifted
maybe today was a struggle
but perhaps tomorrow
i will saddle the elephant
oh and what adventures we shall have.

(*hope*)

this year has taught me,
that happiness is not a destination.
it is a rare fleeting moment
one to behold
close to your heart.
these diamonds in the rough,
are the evanescent glimmer
of a life
worth living.

i've learned
to not let my love for someone
consume me.
nor should i be the sailor
that calms their seas.
they must learn
how to soothe their own storm,
to battle their own sea monsters.
all i can do,
is be their lighthouse,
a flicker of light in the darkness,
a signal of hope still shining.
to be waiting there with a warm embrace,
when they have conquered
their own waves.

sometimes you may feel utterly alone,
you're not.
when it feels as though the world is crumbling apart,
it's not.
your demons will always be with you,
the world will always spin.
so dance with the monsters inside your head,
let the wild fire in your heart
burn the darkness away.
shine as bright as the sun does
when it rises each day.

i let the darkness consume me
in doing so
i uncovered the light
inside of me
is where it grows
now i shall nourish you
ending this internal fight.

we are all quick to admit to
stress or
anxiety
but anxiety is not an emotion.
anxiety is fear.
it's terrifying to admit
that we are so afraid
that we live in fear
it makes us feel weak
but fear is an emotion
emotions tell us things
but sometimes we have learned
from events in our life
to be afraid of things that don't
pose us actual danger.
often
we run, we hide, we avoid
which only causes the fear to grow
keeping us stuck
afraid to leave our minds
even though they are the cause of
this cyclic torture.
we must check the facts.
emotions are not facts.
are we in real danger?
if the answer is no,
then our fear is not justified.
we can confront these demons
for they aren't really monsters
just things we built up in our heads
to be much scarier than they are.

sometimes the pain will hurt worse.
you will especially struggle with this
when you have been through so much more
and survived.
not every pain is the same,
not all heartbreak is equal
although it may seem
like this time
we won't make it
we always survive
we always make it through
because that's just what we do.

today is a better day.
today is better day
than yesterday.
today may be better
than tomorrow,
but that's okay,
because
today is a better day
than yesterday.

　　　{*silver linings*}

the way out.

we often create our own hell
trapped in a mind game of
hellfire & brimstone.
we refuse to accept reality,
the things we fear,
and this keeps us trapped in misery.
we cannot avoid pain
it tells us something is wrong
if we reject our reality
pain transforms into suffering.
the only way out of our own hell
is through our own misery
if we refuse to accept that misery
is the path out of hell
we only fall deeper into our eternal hell.

- radical acceptance is the 1st step

when you notice the red flags
waving in the distance
remember you always have a choice,
don't get caught in a trance
impulse behaviors may be a quick fix
but they only bring guilt
and toxic shame,
a deadly mix.
so listen to your body,
feel your emotions
don't judge them or yourself
don't just go through the motions
choose the things that will
make you happy.
be the one who ends the cyclic cycle
and sets yourself free.

{be your own hero}

when your world falls to chaos
close your eyes
& breathe.
in blue.
out red.
until the world settles around you.

even on good days
my soul aches
for i have risen from the ashes
so many times
i can no longer tell
where the soot begins
& the darkness ends.

i'm working on not emotionally dissociating
and poetry is my way of
connecting with my feelings.
so the walls to my heart
are like that of a sand castle,
constantly being built up
and crumbling down
as the tides change.

write it out.
let everything you hold inside
pour from your soul
until your fingertips run red.
free yourself
from yourself
from your internal torment.

    - the path out of hell

candles burn themselves
to light our world
left a melted mess.
when you care for others
at the expense of yourself
you invite the same fate.

the unfortunate time traveler

i spend my days haunted in the past
                            or manically in the future.
                present is the only time our mind
                and body are in the same place.
                    it's all we really have.

when working on learning
how to create a relationship,
even with yourself,
it's hard to dedicate time
to being with others.
it's okay to take time for yourself
it's not selfish
it's essential.

   {*create healthy boundaries*}

your healing will only ever be about you,
no matter how long it takes
or ugly it may get.
i am a work in progress;
one which requires
no one's seal of approval.
the scars i continue to gain,
bare the marks of battles
i have won in my mind,
my heart and my soul.
i may be damaged,
but i will never be
too broken to fix.

be careful who you choose to love
for if they leave,
they leave a wound as deep
as the love you once had.

today has been a day.
a whirlwind of emotions.
some new, some old.
so i make art
from the broken pieces of my soul,
in hopes that i'll fix this fragmented mess,
or at least heal some of the rest.
i couldn't heal you,
but that doesn't mean
i can't heal myself.

i catch myself catastrophizing
at every upsetting thing.
i have to remind myself,
this is not a crisis.
not every problem has an immediate fix.
not every problem has a solution.

we often lack compassion
when it comes to ourselves.
ask yourself,
if your friend was in the same situation,
what advice would give them?
the shift will surprise you.

- you deserve the same compassion
you give to others

i'm still learning how to let love in,
how to find comfort in touch,
to be soft with myself.

wanting to see the best in someone
doesn't make them into that person.
often it prevents you from seeing the truth.
falling in love with someone
who isn't even real.

{*the figments of our expectations*}

some people are sick in the head,
they don't want to be fixed
but please my dear,
never blame yourself
for their short comings.
insecurity plays a wicked game.

i wish our story was a poem
i could rewrite.
    - there is only acceptance

try as you will
but you can't learn to unlove them,
love always remains.
the true secret to moving on
is learning to love yourself more.

{you are worthy}

i can feel it in my bones
the stirring of something new
the stirring of something not quite ready to bloom
but there is hope in the withered heart of mine
for what grows in this marrow
may be for the very first time,
a love divine.
this might just be,
the love i've been searching for.
could it be?
the love of loving me.

10 A WOLF REBORN

'mentally healthy'
it's the new black
it looks good on everyone.

morning rays
sheets unfrayed
let the light in
today,
let hope win.

self-love is like a delicate flower
not too much sunlight
not too little
just the right amount of water
every. single. day.
every. single. hour.
it's a lot of maintenance.
you won't get it right at first.
your flower may wilt on days.
but one day when you do get the hang of it
you'll cultivate something quite lovely
& when the world is falling apart
you will know your little flower
delicately basking on the windowsill,
will
survive.
for she has grown big heathy roots
with all the care you have invested.
suddenly on bad days
you can now still see color.
color
you now notice
in everyone
in everything.
for in self-love
we find the love of life.

we can only control ourselves,
everything else is just an illusion.

sometimes things happen
that take a lifetime to accept.

finding someone to love you
because you cannot love yourself
will never heal you
it's like putting a band aid on a broken soul,
a hole in your heart,
while the blood still pours out.

smile
even when you can't bear to
smile
even when everything hurts
because
even a broken smile
can heal an aching soul.

i'm nothing
like the girl
you broke.

sometimes
you have to break completely
to find something real.
   - i found me

for most of my life
i have been the witch of my own destruction.
using words to hurt me,
to beat me down.
the pain was comforting,
for it was a spell of my own doing.
if i was already hurting,
no one else could hurt me.
i fed the wolf of darkness
far too much and
far too often,
barely leaving scraps
for the wolf of light.
i let the dark wolf consume me,
feeling powerless to its gluttony,
his hunger only seemed to grow
the more i fed him.
until one day,
i was brave
and asked for help.
now i have learned how to feed the light
the small white wolf inside me grows,
as does my hope to live
rather than just survive.
the dark wolf still begs to be fed
and often it's a reflex for me to do so.
but each day the dark wolf gets smaller as
my wolf of light grows stronger.
it's my choice,
which wolf i feed,
for i am the only one
who can control me.

how big we seem
in our own heads
self-hate, anxiety, depression,
ptsd, disordered eating,
obsession and compulsion.
we forget how tiny we are
in this giant world of beauty
yet discovered.
find your adventure &
lose yourself to the magic
instead of to your own mind.

she finally began to see the light leak out.
and just like that,
she finally allowed herself to fall,
shattering into dust as she hit the floor.
supernova.
from ashes she rises,
a body of gold and light.
she had been so afraid of breaking
she broke herself.
in letting go,
a white wolf emerged.
a new form of beauty
for the world to behold.
but she was no one's.
she finally belonged to herself.

   - finding self-love

find the good in every day,
in every way.

life has made your world
dark-n-stormy.
captain of a ship
with weathered sails & leaky bows.
captain of a ship in need of much repair.
yet a ship like this cannot simply be fixed
for it has witnessed far too much &
survived yet even worse.
the creaks, the cracks, and ragged wear
tell the story of their journeys- who they are.
the storms rage on
& so must the captain and his ship.
never do they know which wave will be their final blow,
which lightning bolt will end them both.
when one has sailed the darkest seas,
one often forgets the light inside them.
the light that has always guided them
through the treacherous rocks
in the darkest of nights.
the light that has always guided them back to shore
once more.
a light that has never dimmed
yet at times is forgotten.
for it's the souls who feel the most darkness
which are graced with the brightest of lights
this is why, time after time
they always find the shore
even when none is within sight.

this world is a scary place my dear
but we are warriors
so let us hold each other's hands
through the dark.
it won't take the darkness away
but we can share this little light
the sparks between us create.

truth or dare.

though it may seem hard to find at times
love is all around us.
it's in the will that gets us out of bed every morning,
holding the door open for a stranger,
the smile and hug when greeting a friend,
taking care of ourselves and others every day.
it may not always be fairytale magic
but love is what we make of it.
just like we are what we make ourselves in to.
so, i dare you,
i dare you to love yourself,
to challenge yourself,
to make your dreams come true.
no matter how impossible they seem
you can always make your passion a reality.
because love
my dear,
is always inside of you.
and that love is all you will ever need.

we do not have to remain broken,
to create great art.
we do not need to remain in pieces,
for others to feel
the beauty we possess.

your mind must accept the things
your heart refuses to.

   - radical acceptance

sometimes we fall in love
with demons,
that doesn't mean
it's never worth
falling in love again.
they can never take away our hope.
oh and what a powerful thing hope is.

no matter who you are
life throws rocks at us all.
we learn together
how to pick up the stones
and build a fortress to live in.

despite all your
broken bits and pieces
you deserve love.
you deserve love
in which you are given
just as much
as you give.

even in her broken smile
her magic still shines.

when one finds themselves
lonely in love
the love is lost
let go
let go
　　- unrequited love of mine

fortified

trauma.
it forces us to break ourselves
down to rubble,
in order to survive.
we aren't even left with
any semblance of self-confidence,
utter loss of ourselves,
for a life
we didn't even want.
what it doesn't teach you
is how to rebuild yourself,
in order to live.
the dust and our spit as tools
to amalgamate what pieces are left.
we may never get them to fit just right
for years and years
clumsily
we struggle.
molding the disheveled parts
in new ways,
until one day they fit,
never just quite right
but enough to let the light shine
on golden seams of the treasure
you have made yourself into.
       - the gleam of hope.

life.
it breaks you down
almost every day at times it seems.
it's the lessons we learn from our mistakes,
preparing us for stormy weather
so when it seems like
you surely can't survive,
you do.
because life has made you sturdy
hardened but with a softness
that understands what it is to bear pain.
there will be days you feel like stone,
numb and cold,
but deep down,
all that you are
is still there
reach into yourself
find the ember that burns inside of you.
all it takes is some blowing to rekindle the flames.
find the things in life that make you feel,
hold them close to you
you are meant to
make this world beautiful.
so burn,
ignite this world
with your shine.

hopeless romantic
with a hopeful heart.

{falling for hope}

i grew a garden
with the tears
of my broken heart
the one you left me with.

{*all life needs broken ground & water to grow*}

all the misery we suffer
a necessary evil.
we are given the choice
to face our demons
or to let them bring us
to our knees.

in the broken cracks
you plowed open
in my heart
i came upon
fertile soil
to sow the seeds
of self-love.
for it was not in
unlearning to love you,
but growing
to love myself more,
which freed my soul
to bloom.

witchcraft

words are my magic.
the makings
of well-crafted spells.
when composed in just the right way
they bring magic to life.
my incantations have the power
to unearth emotions, to save, to process suffering,
to heal, to inspire, to empower
and even cure a lonely soul.
they can conceive light from darkness,
bloom gardens from tears,
create life from death, and
silence our greatest demons.
they can be used for evil or good,
the choice is yours.

i like myself better
when my heart is full of you.

{learning to love myself}

i'll hold on to hope for you
when you no longer can.

Louve -ch

ABOUT THE AUTHOR

*Louve- is a gender nonbinary androgynous poet
who shares her battle with mental health to the world through
her social media presence.
her instagram account @UniqueRadiance,
is iconic for white wild pixie hair, queer style, Louve's two
wolves, and a poem with every post. she brings to light issues
of gender, queer identity and explores many issues people face
but don't often discuss openly.*

Made in the USA
Middletown, DE
04 August 2018